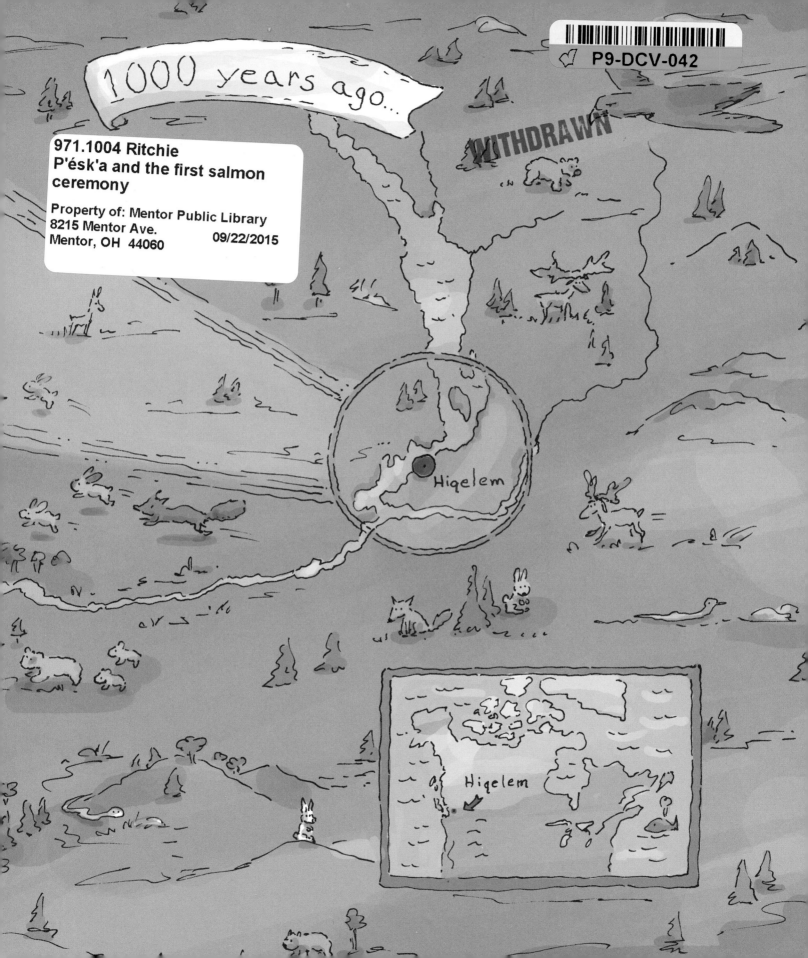

This book is dedicated to the Sts'ailes people.
A big thank you to Morgan Ritchie for all his help.

Copyright © 2015 by Scot Ritchie
Published in Canada and the USA in 2015 by Groundwood Books

Groundwood Books / House of Anansi Press
110 Spadina Avenue, Suite 801, Toronto, Ontario M5V 2K4
or c/o Publishers Group West
1700 Fourth Street, Berkeley, CA 94710

We acknowledge for their financial support of our publishing program the Canada Council for the Arts,
the Government of Canada through the Canada Book Fund (CBF) and the Ontario Arts Council.

**Canada Council
for the Arts**

**Conseil des Arts
du Canada**

**ONTARIO ARTS COUNCIL
CONSEIL DES ARTS DE L'ONTARIO**
an Ontario government agency
un organisme du gouvernement de l'Ontario

Library and Archives Canada Cataloguing in Publication
Ritchie, Scot, author
P'ésk'a and the first salmon ceremony / written and illustrated
by Scot Ritchie.
Issued in print and electronic formats.
ISBN 978-1-55498-718-4 (bound).—ISBN 978-1-55498-719-1 (pdf)
1. Chehalis Indians—Social life and customs—Juvenile literature.
2. Chehalis Indians—Fishing—Juvenile literature. 3. Salmon fishing—
Juvenile literature. I. Title.
E99.C49R58 2015   j971.1004'9794   C2015-900106-4
                         C2015-900107-2

The illustrations were first drawn in pencil, followed by fine line work in ink. They were then
scanned into the computer and colored in Photoshop.
Printed and bound in Malaysia

MIX
Paper from
responsible sources
FSC® C012700

P'ésk'a
and the
First Salmon
Ceremony

SCOT RITCHIE

GROUNDWOOD BOOKS
HOUSE OF ANANSI PRESS
TORONTO BERKELEY

What if you could go back in time?

P'ésk'a opens his eyes. Today is an important day for his people — the Sts'ailes. But the special tray needed for the ceremony has been left behind!

With the tray under his arm, P'ésk'a goes
looking for the Siyá:m — the chief.

Every spring P'ésk'a's people celebrate the
First Salmon Ceremony. It's their way of saying
thank you to the river for all the salmon it
brings.

Salmon is the most important food for the Sts'ailes people, but P'ésk'a and his family also rely on other animals and berries to eat. Everything the Sts'ailes need to survive is found in the forest and the river.

These men have cut down a cedar tree to make a canoe. First, the trunk is hollowed out. Then, hot rocks and boiling water are placed inside, and the trunk is steamed over the fire to change its shape.

P'ésk'a is going to make his own canoe when he is older.

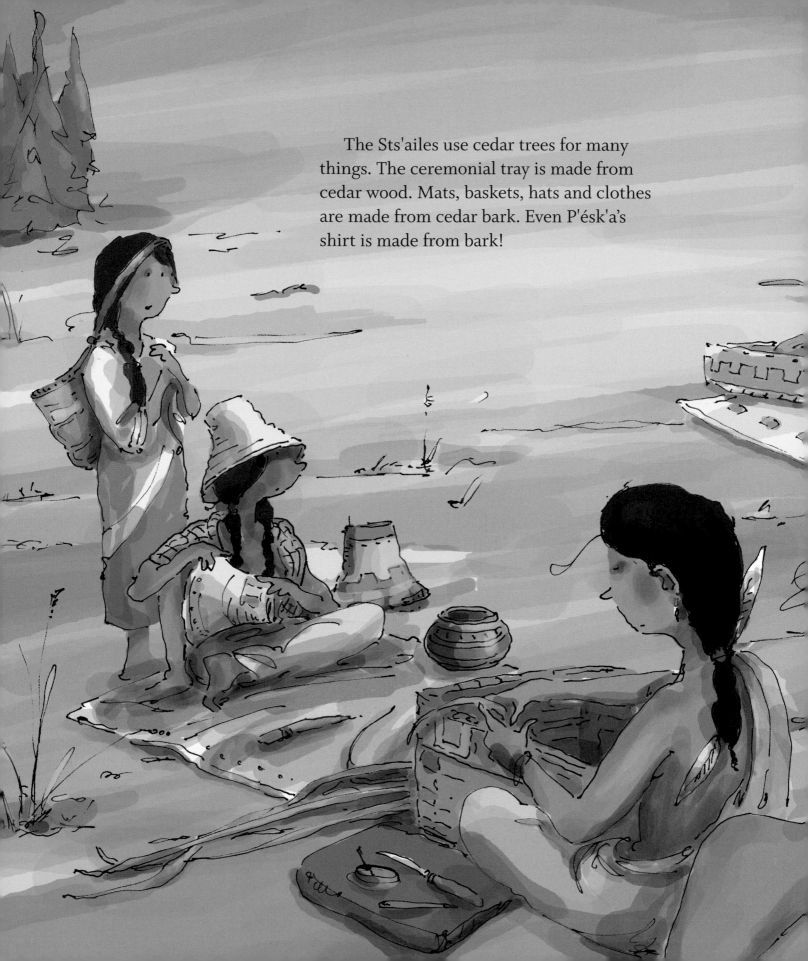

The Sts'ailes use cedar trees for many things. The ceremonial tray is made from cedar wood. Mats, baskets, hats and clothes are made from cedar bark. Even P'ésk'a's shirt is made from bark!

Everything smells so good that
P'ésk'a has to stop for a minute at
the smokehouse to catch his breath.
Smoked salmon and dried blueberries
are his favorite foods, but today there's
no time for a snack.

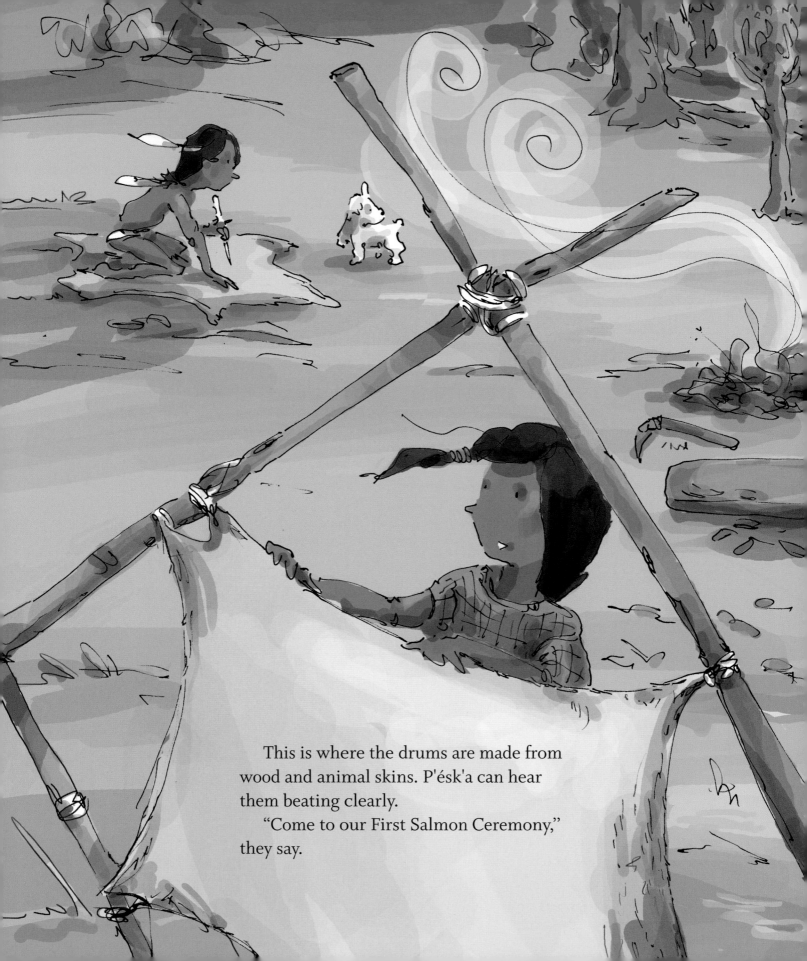

This is where the drums are made from
wood and animal skins. P'ésk'a can hear
them beating clearly.
"Come to our First Salmon Ceremony,"
they say.

Bang! Bang! The ceremony starts when the
first salmon is caught and put over the fire.
There is more than enough for everyone.
  P'ésk'a runs to the chief and delivers the
ceremonial tray, just in time.

What a feast!

The people have finished eating, and they
put the salmon bones on the ceremonial tray.
The chief leads the procession. With a splash,
he returns the salmon bones to the river.

Everybody thanks the river for the sth'óqwi
— the greatest gift.

More About the Sts'ailes People

The Sts'ailes live on the Harrison River today, as they have for at least the past ten thousand years. All the ancient buildings are long gone, but if you visit, you can see where P'ésk'a ran through the village to deliver his tray.

Art was important to the Sts'ailes. It reminded them who their ancestors were. It was used for decoration on drums, clothes and baskets.

The wooly dog shown in the story was only found in this area of North America and is now extinct. Fur from these dogs was woven into blankets and clothing.

Everybody was related and many families lived together in pit houses or plank houses. Plank houses were bigger.

To make a pit house, digging sticks were used to loosen the earth. Then large pieces of wood served as shovels. This was a community effort involving twenty or more people.

Nobody knows for sure, but it is believed that one thousand years ago the population of Hiqelem was about five hundred people. There were fourteen pit houses and six plank houses.

Rocks, bones and wood were used to make things like spears, arrows and paddles.

Salmon were prepared in many ways. Some were eaten fresh, some cooked over the fire, some wind-dried, some smoked over the fire, and others cooked in underground ovens.

To bring down the giant cedar trees, the Sts'ailes used an adze (a combination of an ax and a chisel) and hot rocks. A hole was carved in the trunk of a tree so a heated rock could be placed inside to singe the wood. When the wood was soft enough, it was removed using the adze. This was repeated until the tree fell down.

Glossary

The Sts'ailes language was banned at one time, but people are learning it again thanks to community elders and teachers. Here are some words you might want to learn.

Chá:lhtel (chahl-tl) – to smoke fish
P'ésk'a (peskahh) – hummingbird
Sátet (satet) – to offer something or pass it along
Sítel (seetall) – basket
Siyá:m (she-am) – chief
Sméq'eth (smekoth) – gift of leftover food for guests
    to take home
Sqémél (skumel) – pit house
Sqwemá:y (skwamaih) – dog
Sth'óqwi (stow-kwey) – salmon, fish
Stó:lō (stahlo) – river people
Sts'ailes (stehles) – beating heart
Tál (tel) – mother

A Letter from Chief William Charlie
of the Sts'ailes People

Dear Readers,

I am pleased to see this book, which helps bring to life the ancient life of our people. The Sts'ailes are actively revitalizing our history, language and culture through education, both for our own people and for others, and this book will be a valuable tool in this ongoing effort.

Scot Ritchie's artistic expression of Sts'ailes life and culture is based on careful research and is also very respectfully executed. I am glad that it will be available for children from all places to read.

For those who want to learn more, Sts'ailes is a warm and welcoming community. Maybe some day you will visit us!

Chief William Charlie

Hiqelem